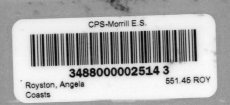

DATE DUE

My World of Geography
COASTS

Angela Royston
Heinemann Library
Chicago, Illinois

© 2005 Heinemann Library
a division of Reed Elsevier Inc.
Chicago, Illinois

Customer Service 888-454-2279
Visit our website at www.heinemannlibrary.com

Design: Ron Kamen and Celia Jones
Illustrations: Jo Brooker (p. 17), Jeff Edwards
  (p. 5), Art Construction and Darrell Warner (pp. 28–29)
Photo Research: Rebecca Sodergren, Melissa Allison, and
  Debra Weatherley
Originated by Ambassador Litho
Printed and bound in Hong Kong and China by South
China Printing

09 08 07 06 05
10 9 8 7 6 5 4 3 2 1

**Library of Congress
Cataloging-in-Publication Data**
Royston, Angela.
  Coasts / Angela Royston.
     p. cm. – (My world of geography)
  Includes bibliographical references and index.
  ISBN 1-4034-5595-3
  1. Coasts–Juvenile literature. I. Title. II. Series.
  GB453.R69 2005
  551.45'7–dc22

                          2004003863

Acknowledgments
The author and publisher are grateful to the following for
permission to reproduce copyright material:
pp. 4, 8, 9 (Brandon D. Cole), 10 (David Muench), 11
(Kevin Morris), 14 (Neil Rabinowitz), 16 (Bill Ross), 19
(Yan Arthus-Bertrand), 21 (Macduff Everton), 22, 23 (Tony
Arruza) Corbis; pp. 6, 12, 25 Getty Images/Photodisc;
pp. 7, 13 (Jon Wilson) Science Photo Library; p. 15 (Dave
Newbould) Photo Library Wales; p. 18 (Dr. B. Booth)
Geoscience Features; pp. 20 (Quentin Bates), 27 (Erik
Schaffer) Ecoscene; p. 24 (Guy Mansfield) Panos Pictures;
p. 26 (Ray Pfortner) Still Pictures.

Cover photograph reproduced with permission of Corbis.

Every effort has been made to contact copyright holders of
any material reproduced in this book. Any omissions will
be rectified in subsequent printings if notice is given to the
publisher.

Contents

What Is a Coast? 4
Beaches 6
Rocks 8
Salty Swamps. 10
Waves 12
Caves and Bays 14
Ragged Coasts. 16
Forming New Land 18
Food from the Seashore 20
Ports and Harbors. 22
Enjoying the Seashore 24
Coasts in Danger 26
Facts About Coasts 28
Glossary 30
More Books to Read 31
Index 32

Some words are shown in bold, **like this.** You can find out what they mean by looking in the glossary.

What Is a Coast?

A coast is land that lies next to the ocean or sea. Oceans and seas cover most of Earth. **Seashores** and **beaches** are places where seawater splashes against land.

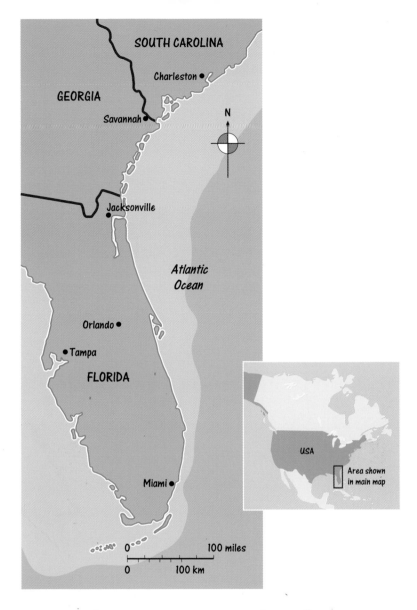

This map shows a stretch of coast.
On a map the sea is usually colored
blue. Deep water is a darker blue.
The land is colored green or brown.

Beaches

Some **beaches** are covered with sand. Sometimes the wind blows the sand into hills called **dunes.** Other beaches are covered with mud. Worms and **shellfish** live on sandy and muddy beaches.

sand dunes

sand

Some beaches are covered with **pebbles** or shells. Not many animals live on pebbly beaches.

Rocks

Many parts of the coast have no **beach.** The **seashore** is just bare rock. Sometimes steep **cliffs** separate the land from the sea.

rock

cliff

Many kinds of animals live on rocky **seashores.** Some live in **rock pools.** Others cling to the rocks. Different kinds of **seaweed** cling to the rocks, too.

seaweed

starfish

Starfish, sea anemones, and seaweed live in this rock pool.

sea anemone

9

Salty Swamps

A **swamp** is an area of wet, soggy land. In some places on the coast, the sea **floods** part of the land. This turns the land into a salty swamp.

Most plants cannot grow in salty water. But in hot places, mangrove trees grow well in salty swamps. **Roots** grow down from the tree branches into the swamp.

roots

11

Waves

Waves hit the **seashore** all the time. When the sea is stormy, the waves are bigger and more powerful.

Waves slowly wear away the rocks and **cliffs.** The rocks crack and crumble to form large stones, **pebbles,** and sand.

pebbles

As the waves crash onto the seashore, the pebbles rub against each other and become round and smooth.

Caves and Bays

Some rocks are hard. Other rocks are soft. The sea wears away soft rocks faster than hard rocks. A **cave** forms when waves wear away an area of soft rock in a **cliff.**

cave

A **bay** forms where the sea wears away a long stretch of soft rock. The hard rock on each side wears away much more slowly. It sticks out into the sea and forms a **headland.**

headlands

bays

Ragged Coasts

A coast forms the edge of the land. A ragged coast has many **headlands** and **bays.** A headland sticks out into the sea. A bay lets the sea go farther inland.

Key

land

bay

buildings

sea

headland

This map shows the same area of coast as the photo on page 16. You can see the shape of the coast made by the headlands and the bays. You can draw a map like this.

Forming New Land

Sometimes the sea sweeps sand and **pebbles** from one part of the coast to another. As the sand and pebbles pile up, new land forms.

This lighthouse used to be at the edge of the sea.

spit

Rivers also help build new land at the
seashore. Rivers carry soil and
stones into the sea. If the sea is
shallow, the soil and stones pile up
to form a **spit.**

Food from the Seashore

Many **shellfish** live on the **seashore.** People catch shellfish to eat. They gather shellfish such as mussels, crabs, and lobsters.

This special basket for catching lobsters is called a lobster pot.

Many kinds of fish live in the sea close to the seashore. People catch fish with rods or nets. This boy has caught shrimp in his net.

Ports and Harbors

Some towns and cities are built along the **seashore.** A **port** is a town or city where ships can load and unload **goods. Docks** are places where ships can drop anchor.

Cranes load and unload goods from big ships.

harbor

pier

A **harbor** is part of the seashore that is sheltered from the wind and waves. Sometimes people build a **pier** to make the water in the harbor even more sheltered.

Enjoying the Seashore

Many towns on the coast are vacation spots. People go to these towns to enjoy the **seashore.** Some coastal towns have sandy **beaches** where people swim.

Some people go to coastal towns to enjoy windsurfing and sailing. Other people go to the seashore to surf on the large waves.

Coasts in Danger

People are damaging the **seashore.** In some places, **waste** from homes and **factories** flows into the sea. The waste **pollutes** the sea and washes onto the **beach.**

The sea is wearing away some parts of the seashore. The people who lived in the houses on the edge of this **cliff** had to leave their homes.

Facts About Coasts

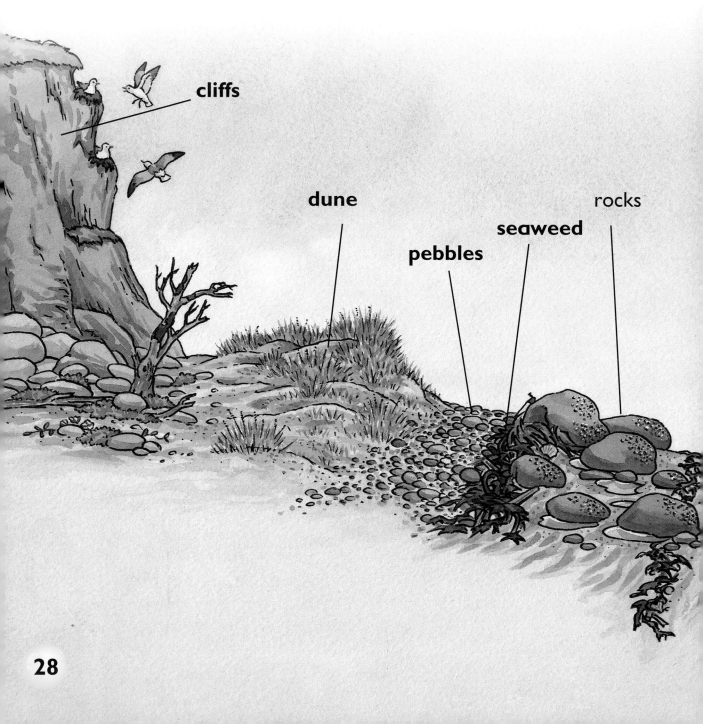

cliffs

dune

pebbles

seaweed

rocks

This picture shows some of the
different things you might find on a
seashore. The level of the sea
changes during the day. This is called
the tide. The highest level is high tide.
The lowest level is low tide.

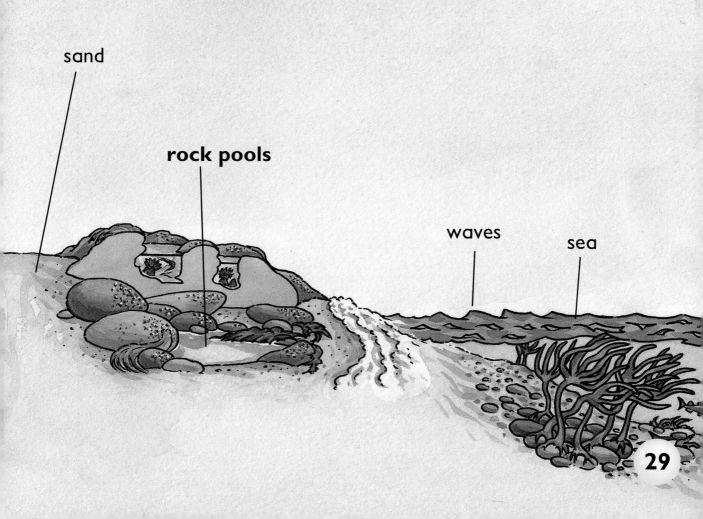

sand

rock pools

waves

sea

Glossary

bay part of the coastline where the sea flows farther inland

beach stretch of seashore covered by sand, mud, pebbles, or shells

cave large hole or hollow

cliff very steep slope

dock concrete platform built in a harbor where ships can unload

dune hill of sand

factory place where people make things

flood fill with water

goods things that are made, bought, and sold

harbor sheltered part of the sea at the coast where boats can load and unload

headland piece of land that sticks out into the sea

pebble round, smooth stone on the seashore

pier large platform or wall built into the sea

pollute damage something by making it dirty

port town or city where ships load and unload

rock pool pool of salty water among the rocks on a beach

root part of a plant that takes in water from the soil

seashore flat area of land next to the sea or ocean

seaweed plant that grows in the sea

shallow not deep

shellfish animal that has a shell and lives in water

spit strip of new land that forms at some places on the coast

swamp wet, soggy ground

waste leftover materials that people do not want

More Books to Read

Ashwell, Miranda, and Andy Owen. *Seas and Oceans.* Chicago: Heinemann Library, 1998.

Galko, Francine. *Coral Reef Animals.* Chicago: Heinemann Library, 2003.

Galko, Francine. *Sea Animals.* Chicago: Heinemann Library, 2003.

Galko, Francine. *Seashore Animals.* Chicago: Heinemann Library, 2003.

Hewitt, Sally. *Rivers, Ponds, and Seashore.* New York: Millbrook Press, 1999.

Llewellyn, Claire. *Caves.* Chicago: Heinemann Library, 2001.

Llewellyn, Claire. *Coral Reefs.* Chicago: Heinemann Library, 2001.

Wilkes, Angela. *The Seashore: Explore and Discover.* Boston: Houghton Mifflin, 2001.

Index

animals 6–7, 9, 20–21

bays 15, 16, 17
beaches 4, 6–7, 8, 24, 26

caves 14
cliffs 8, 13, 14, 27

docks 22
dunes 6

enjoying the seashore 24–25

fishing 20, 21
flooding 10

harbors 23
headlands 15, 16, 17

mangrove trees 11
maps 5, 17

new land formation 18–19

pebbles 7, 13, 18
piers 23
plants 9, 11

pollution 26
ports 22
protecting the seashore 26–27

ragged coasts 16–17
rivers 19
rock pools 9
rocks 8–9, 13, 14, 15

sand 6, 13, 18
sea 4, 5, 10, 14, 15, 16, 18, 27
seashore 4, 8, 12, 19, 20, 22, 23, 24, 26, 28
seaweed 9
shellfish 7, 20, 21
spits 19
swamps 10–11

tides 28
towns and cities 22, 24

water sports 25
waves 12–13, 14, 23